Little People, BIG DREAMS
DAVID BOWIE

Written by
Mª Isabel Sánchez Vegara

Illustrated by
Ana Albero

Frances Lincoln
Children's Books

Little David lived with his family in a tiny house, on an ordinary street, in London. But he had ideas that would take him out of this world.

At school, he loved music and dance classes.
He had a real talent for singing and his dance moves
were from another planet. His teachers had never seen
anything like it before.

He spent hours listening to his brother's rock and jazz records. David was so inspired by the power of music that he started to write his own songs.

David studied art, music, and design at school.
Sometimes his teachers were not sure if he was a boy
or a girl, but David was just delighted to be himself.

One day, he got into a silly fight with his friend George, who punched him in the eye. That punch changed David's look forever, and made him strangely magnetic.

David and George remained friends and formed a group called the Konrads. The rest of the band was happy playing at weddings, but David wanted to become a star.

He jumped from band to band looking for
a chance, dreaming that—one day—all the lonely
kids on planet Earth would sing his songs out loud.

But David knew that a great singer needed to be a great performer, too. He decided to mix his music with the most spectacular outfits and dance moves ever seen onstage.

David wrote a song about a lonely astronaut, and it became his first big hit. The whole world listened to his song the day man first walked on the moon.

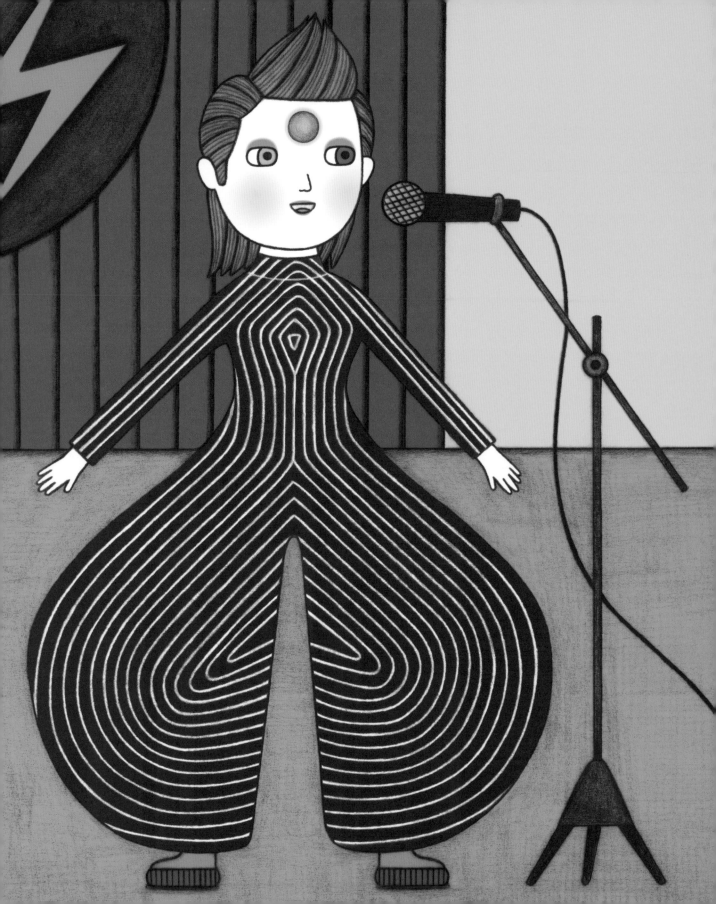

Next, David transformed into an alien rock star called Ziggy Stardust, the coolest space invader the world had ever seen. Dressed as Ziggy, he finally made it to superstardom.

David wasn't sure where he was going from there, but he knew it wouldn't be boring. He kept reinventing himself—and that's what made him David Bowie.

For more than 40 years, he kept exploring new galaxies.
Filled with futuristic sounds, he inspired generations of fans
to find their own voice and dare to be different.

And by never being afraid to be himself, little David became the most unique star who ever fell to Earth.

DAVID BOWIE

(Born 1947 • Died 2016)

c. 1960

1973

David Bowie was born David Jones in Brixton, London. From an early age, he loved to express himself through music, dance, and painting. His older brother, Terry, introduced him to music records, and David was hooked. He started to learn many instruments, including the saxophone. In 1962, his friend George punched him in the eye, which left him with a permanently dilated pupil. This made his eyes look like they were different colors, as his left pupil was so big. After a four-month stint in the hospital, and multiple surgeries, George and David made up, and formed their first band: the Konrads. They played weddings and small events, but David wanted to be a star. He left school at 16, deciding to take his musical career to the next level. He played with many bands and changed his name to David Bowie to stand out. Bowie went solo and his

1976   c. 1995

career rocketed: his songs became household tunes. His first hit "Space Oddity" was played on television over the Apollo 11 moon landing. Bowie then imagined himself as a new character, Ziggy Stardust. He adopted a character with a red quiff, face paint, and wild outfits. His song "Changes" came to represent how David reinvented himself and his music. He was a style chameleon, whose songs hopped across genres and were influenced by artists like Andy Warhol. From pop to rock, David continued to make music until he passed away from cancer, in 2016. Many people thought that his last album, *Blackstar*, was a final, knowing gift to his fans. Over his lifetime, David made 26 albums, was entered into the Rock and Roll Hall of Fame, and won the Grammy Lifetime Achievement Award. He left the world as one of the most iconic singer-songwriters of his generation.

Want to find out more about **David Bowie?**
Read one of these great books and listen to these songs:

The People Awards by Lily Murray and Ana Albero

Bowie A to Z by Steve Wide and Libby Vanderploeg (for older readers)

"Starman" and "Space Oddity" by David Bowie

If you're in Brixton, London, you could visit the David Bowie wall mural and leave some flowers.

BOARD BOOKS

COCO CHANEL

ISBN: 978-1-78603-245-4

MAYA ANGELOU

ISBN: 978-1-78603-249-2

FRIDA KAHLO

ISBN: 978-1-78603-247-8

AMELIA EARHART

ISBN: 978-1-78603-252-2

MARIE CURIE

ISBN: 978-1-78603-253-9

ADA LOVELACE

ISBN:978-1-78603-259-1

ROSA PARKS

ISBN: 978-1-78603-263-8

EMMELINE PANKHURST

ISBN: 978-1-78603-261-4

AUDREY HEPBURN

ISBN: 978-1-78603-255-3

ELLA FITZGERALD

ISBN:978-1-78603-257-7

BOOKS & PAPER DOLLS

EMMELINE PANKHURST

MARIE CURIE

ISBN: 978-1-78603-400-7   ISBN: 978-1-78603-401-4

BOX SETS

WOMEN IN ART

WOMEN IN SCIENCE

ISBN: 978-1-78603-428-1   ISBN: 978-1-78603-429-8

Collect the *Little People*, **BIG DREAMS** series:

FRIDA KAHLO

ISBN: 978-1-84780-783-0

COCO CHANEL

ISBN: 978-1-84780-784-7

MAYA ANGELOU

ISBN: 978-1-84780-889-9

AMELIA EARHART
ISBN: 978-1-84780-888-2

AGATHA CHRISTIE

ISBN: 978-1-84780-960-5

MARIE CURIE

ISBN: 978-1-84780-962-9

ROSA PARKS

ISBN: 978-1-78603-018-4

AUDREY HEPBURN

ISBN: 978-1-78603-053-5

EMMELINE PANKHURST

ISBN: 978-1-78603-020-7

ELLA FITZGERALD

ISBN: 978-1-78603-087-0

ADA LOVELACE

ISBN: 978-1-78603-076-4

JANE AUSTEN

ISBN: 978-1-78603-120-4

GEORGIA O'KEEFFE

ISBN: 978-1-78603-122-8

HARRIET TUBMAN
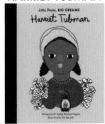
ISBN: 978-1-78603-227-0

ANNE FRANK

ISBN: 978-1-78603-229-4

MOTHER TERESA

ISBN: 978-1-78603-230-0

JOSEPHINE BAKER

ISBN: 978-1-78603-228-7

L. M. MONTGOMERY

ISBN: 978-1-78603-233-1

JANE GOODALL

ISBN: 978-1-78603-231-7

SIMONE DE BEAUVOIR

ISBN: 978-1-78603-232-4

MUHAMMAD ALI
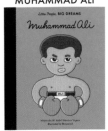
ISBN: 978-1-78603-331-4

STEPHEN HAWKING

ISBN: 978-1-78603-333-8

MARIA MONTESSORI

ISBN: 978-1-78603-755-8

VIVIENNE WESTWOOD

ISBN: 978-1-78603-757-2

MAHATMA GANDHI

ISBN: 978-1-78603-787-9

Brimming with creative inspiration, how-to projects, and useful information to enrich your everyday life, Quarto Knows is a favorite destination for those pursuing their interests and passions. Visit our site and dig deeper with our books into your area of interest: Quarto Creates, Quarto Cooks, Quarto Homes, Quarto Lives, Quarto Drives, Quarto Explores, Quarto Gifts, or Quarto Kids.

First Published in the UK in 2019 by Frances Lincoln Children's Books, an imprint of The Quarto Group.

400 First Avenue North, Suite 400, Minneapolis, MN 55401, USA.

T (612) 344-8100 F (612) 344-8692 **www.QuartoKnows.com**

First Published in Spain in 2019 under the title Pequeña & Grande David Bowie

by Alba Editorial, s.l.u., Baixada de Sant Miquel, 1, 08002 Barcelona

www.albaeditorial.es

A catalog record for this book is available from the British Library.

ISBN 978-1-78603-332-1

The illustrations were created in pencil and colored digitally.

Set in Futura BT.

Published by Rachel Williams • Designed by Karissa Santos

Edited by Katy Flint • Production by Jenny Cundill

Manufactured in Guangdong, China CC022019

9 7 5 3 1 2 4 6 8

Photographic acknowledgments (pages 28–29, from left to right) 1. Photo of David BOWIE; Davie Jones (Davy Jones), posed portrait, c. 1960 © CA/Redferns.com via Getty Images 2. David Bowie (1947–2016) performs on stage on his Ziggy Stardust/Aladdin Sane tour in London, 1973. © Michael Putland via Getty Images 3. David Bowie poses for a portrait, 1976. © Masayoshi Sukita/RCA/ via Getty Images 4. English musician, singer-songwriter, and actor David Bowie with his wife Somali fashion model Iman, c. 1995 © Rose Hartman via Getty Images